Drowning in a Bottle

TEENS AND ALCOHOL ABUSE

by Gail B. Stewart

Content Adviser:
Billy AraJeJe Woods, Ph.D.,
Department of Psychology, Saddleback College,
Mission Viejo, California

Reading Adviser:
Rosemary G. Palmer, Ph.D.,
Department of Literacy, College of Education,
Boise State University

Compass Point Books
151 Good Counsel Drive
P.O. Box 669
Mankato, MN 56002-0669

 This book was manufactured with paper containing
at least 10 percent post-consumer waste.

Photographs ©: Capstone Press/Karon Dubke, cover; iStockphoto/phlegma,
5, Jesper Wittorff, 7, Paul Vasarhelyi, 14, Judi Ashlock, 22, Sean Locke,
30, Khuong Hoang, 39; Alamy/Kuttig-People, 8, David Young-Wolff, 9,
Richard Levine, 13, ACE STOCK LIMITED, 16, Bubbles Photolibrary/
Angela Hampton, 17, Jack Sullivan, 19, 39, Olaf Doering, 23, Mira, 40 (right);
Shutterstock/Monkey Business Images, 10, 42, Natalia D. , 27, Dean Mitchell,
33; Getty Images Inc./Photographer's Choice/Simon Battensby, 11, Taxi, 20,
Stone/David Young-Wolff, 29; Corbis/Randy Faris, 24; PhotoEdit Inc./Richard
Hutchings, 35, Mary Kate Denny, 37, 38; AP Images/*The Herald and News*/Ron
Winn, 40, (left).

For Compass Point Books
Brenda Haugen, Heidi Thompson, Jo Miller, LuAnn Ascheman-Adams,
Joe Ewest, Nick Healy, and Catherine Neitge

For Bow Publications
Bonnie Szumski, Kim Turner, and Katy Harlowe

Library of Congress Cataloging-in-Publication Data
Stewart, Gail B. (Gail Barbara), 1949–
Drowning in a bottle : teens and alcohol abuse / by Gail B. Stewart.
p. cm.—(What's the issue?)
Includes index.
ISBN 978-0-7565-4151-4 (library binding)
1. Teenagers—Alcohol use—Alcoholism—United States—Juvenile literature.
3. Drinking of alcoholic beverages—United States—Juvenile literature.
I. Title. II. Series.
HV5135.S754 2009
362.292'208350973—dc2   2008040355

Visit Compass Point Books on the Internet at *www.compasspointbooks.com*
or e-mail your request to *custserv@compasspointbooks.com*

TABLE OF CONTENTS

CHAPTER one

WHAT'S THE BIG DEAL ABOUT DRINKING?

The party started out great. The music was loud, and everyone was having fun. There were big ice-filled tubs with plenty of beer. Nora* was especially glad that everyone she'd invited (and maybe even a few more) had come.

But two more people arrived at midnight when the party was really at full swing. These were people Nora was sure were going to be out of town—her mother and father. And they were furious at what their 14-year-old daughter and her friends had done.

* In this book, names have been changed to protect the privacy of people involved, except in cases where names were reported in the media.

"It was bad," remembers Nora, now a 19-year-old college student. "My dad was so mad it seemed like he had smoke coming out of his ears. The house was really trashed. There were cigarette butts and beer cans everywhere. One girl had gone into my parents' room and passed out on their bed. There were cigarette burns on the couch in the den. Somebody had thrown up in the hallway, and everything smelled horrible."

"My dad was so mad it seemed like he had smoke coming out of his ears. The house was really trashed."

Nora still feels terrible about that night. "I know it could have been way worse," she says. "I mean, someone could have gotten in their car drunk and killed somebody—or themselves.

It doesn't matter where you drink—in a bar, at home, or at a friend's party. In the United States it's illegal for anyone under 21 to drink.

But still, it was absolutely the stupidest thing I've ever done. But when you're in high school, you don't always think so clearly."

Alcohol Everywhere

Today drinking is part of our culture. Sometimes it's offering a champagne toast to the happy couple at a wedding. Or it's taking a bottle of wine to the host of a dinner party. Sometimes it's just enjoying a cold beer at a ball game.

Despite the widespread acceptance of alcohol in society, the law still restricts who can drink. In the United States, you have to be at least 21 to buy or drink alcohol. But for many teens, this law is simply ignored. There are more than 11 million underage drinkers in the United States, according to a 2007 U.S. Surgeon General's report. About 3 million of those are alcohol abusers, or heavy drinkers.

One thing that a lot of teens— and even a lot of adults—don't think about is that alcohol is a drug. Actually it's the most commonly used drug in the world. Even though it's a beverage made from grapes (such as wine) or grain (such as beer), it has no food value. It's a drug because of how it affects your body—especially your brain.

Do you know how potentially dangerous a drug it is? Alcohol kills more than 100,000 Americans each year. Many of those deaths are due to drunk driving or other types of accidents. Some young people die from binge drinking, or drinking too much in a short time. In other cases, years of drinking can cause cancer, stroke, and fatal liver disease.

But it's not just adult drinkers who are at risk. An average of 5,000 people under the age of 21 die because of alcohol each year, according to the Centers for Disease Control. More than

A Real Disease

Alcoholism is a chronic disease, which means it lasts a person's entire life. Whether a person develops this disease is influenced by that person's lifestyle and genes—basic units of heredity that are passed on to offspring from parents. But just because someone may be at risk of developing the disease because of family history does *not* mean he or she is destined to become an alcoholic. And some people become alcoholics even though no one else in their family has the disease.

145,000 emergency room visits by people between 12 and 21 years old are alcohol-related, too. For American teens, alcohol is their favorite drug of choice, says U.S. Surgeon General Kenneth Moritsugu. Just a beverage? No way.

Twenty-eight percent of 15- to 20-year-old drivers killed in motor vehicle crashes in 2005 had been drinking.

The average age for experimenting with alcohol for the first time is 11 for boys and 13 for girls.

Too Many Kids

The problem with alcohol is that it can be easily abused no matter how old you are. And this is the scary part for kids: The earlier you start drinking, the more likely you are to become addicted. In fact, experts say that kids who start drinking before age 15 are five times more likely to become alcoholics than those who start at age 21.

Jerry fits right into that category. He began drinking when he was 13. He says, "I was hurting all the time. My family was really messed up. My mother used drugs and really wasn't available to us kids. I never felt good, or right, about anything.

Why 21?

The minimum age at which you can legally drink alcohol in the United States is 21, but it hasn't always been that way. During the Vietnam War, many 18 year olds were drafted into the military. These same 18 year olds could not drink alcohol legally. Many of these young people protested that they could fight and die for their country but couldn't legally drink beer, or vote, for that matter. This argument made sense to many lawmakers, and many voted to lower the drinking age in their states. Twenty-nine states lowered the drinking age—many to as low as 18. But by 1984, experts had noticed that more teens were involved in fatal driving accidents. That year, the federal government enacted the Uniform Drinking Age Act, which reduced federal transportation funds to states refusing to raise the drinking age to 21.

Alcohol helped me stop thinking about it. I was able to relax and forget. I didn't realize that it wouldn't help me get better in the long run. In fact, drinking became a life-long problem."

"I didn't realize that it wouldn't help me get better in the long run. In fact, drinking became a life-long problem."

Corey says he was a young drinker, too. "My dad had a refrigerator out in the garage and stocked it with beer. My friend and I used to go out there when no one was around and drink a couple beers each. We

You might feel as if you're the only teen who chooses not to drink, but you're not. Groups such as Students Against Destructive Decisions work hard to help their classmates make good choices.

Many teens have easy access to alcohol. They often can find it at home.

started that back in like fourth grade. I've been drinking ever since. But that's how it started for me."

Earlier and Earlier

Stories like Corey's and Jerry's are not unusual. In fact, 3 million U.S. teenagers are alcohol abusers. Millions more drink regularly. "The problem [with underage drinking] is how young kids are starting now," says Martha Nelson, who works with teen alcohol users. "We're seeing kids now as young as 11 or 12 using [alcohol] on a regular basis."

CHAPTER two

"I JUST WANTED TO BE DRUNK"

Many adults can enjoy one or two drinks in a social context. For adults who drink occasionally, a glass of wine or a beer or a mixed drink of hard liquor is a way to relax.

Theo, a bartender, says that's true of most of his customers. "They'll order a drink and kick back with their friends after work," he says. "They make it last a half hour or so, just unwind. They like the relaxed feeling. They like the taste. That's all there is to it."

But many adults and teens cannot drink alcohol in a casual way. For them, drinking becomes compulsive. Teens may drink too much just to fit in with other teens who are drinking. Or they may use alcohol to excess to block out their problems.

Businesses face serious legal consequences if they serve alcohol to those who are underage.

"That's what it was in my case," says Corey. "I just wanted to be drunk."

Corey is sober now but says that he started drinking regularly when he was 10 years old. "It wasn't the taste—it all tasted lousy to me. It was all about how much I could drink and how fast I could get wasted. That was the goal. That way I didn't have to

"It wasn't the taste—it all tasted lousy to me. It was all about how much I could drink and how fast I could get wasted."

think about my parents fighting all the time."

Your Body Is Smart

Alcohol is a mild toxin, or

Drinking Is Not a Beauty Secret

Drinking not only harms your health, it has an effect on your appearance:

- **Drinking dries out your skin, making you look old before your time.**

- **As you drink, blood vessels in your face get smaller, causing redness and blotchiness on your cheeks, nose, and eyes.**

- **You almost always gain weight when you drink. A mixed drink like a margarita has 400 calories or more. You don't feel full after you have alcohol, so you often eat more when drinking.**

poison. When you drink, your body recognizes that it isn't good for you. As a result, your body doesn't digest the alcohol but instead tries to get rid of it as fast as possible. As soon as you begin drinking, the alcohol is absorbed into the bloodstream quickly. This is your body's attempt to process the alcohol.

Once it gets to your bloodstream, the alcohol travels

Drinking alone is a sign of a possible alcohol problem.

throughout your body. When the alcohol gets to your brain, it slows down your central nervous system, which affects your heart rate and your breathing. If you're drinking a small amount, you'll have a relaxed feeling.

It takes about 40 minutes for the body to burn off one drink—a 12-ounce (360-milliliter) beer, 1.5 ounces (45 mL) of hard liquor in a mixed drink, or a 5-ounce (150-mL) glass of wine, for example. If you have a second drink, and a third after that, your body just can't keep up. That's what getting drunk is—drinking so much that your body can't burn it off fast enough. When that happens, you see some pretty startling effects.

Being Drunk

Of course, the changes in your body can vary depending on how much you weigh, whether you had anything to eat before you began drinking, and so on. But let's say you weigh between 110 and 130 pounds (50 and 59 kilograms). After two drinks, your speech may become slurred. You feel lightheaded, too.

After a third drink, you have trouble keeping your balance. You may stagger instead of walk.

Watch Out ... Blackout

One of the most frightening things that can happen when you drink too much is called a blackout. It's not the same as passing out or losing consciousness. Basically, the alcohol creates a situation in your brain where you cannot remember anything that happened to you during a given time. The time elapsed may be a few minutes or hours. Some alcoholics can be awake and functioning for days but have no memory of it. Experts say that even under hypnosis, people can never remember what went on during a blackout.

You may begin to feel nauseated. You have difficulty talking, and you have trouble remembering things, such as names of people and your address. Your body may try to rid itself of the alcohol by vomiting. But even then, the effects of the alcohol are still present in your behavior.

Being drunk changes not only your speech and balance, but also how you act. Some people become mean and angry when they drink too much. They may lash out at friends or perfect strangers.

They may swear or call people ugly names they would never use if they were sober. And they have no idea that they've done anything wrong. That little voice inside that tells us we're making a bad decision disappears.

I Did What?

Not everyone who gets drunk becomes mean or angry. A person who is usually shy may use alcohol to feel less inhibited. But instead of being just a bit more outgoing, several drinks can

People's reactions to alcohol vary greatly. Some people become quiet and depressed, while others get angry and may even get in fights.

Parental Involvement

Forty percent of underage drinkers say they get their alcohol from an adult— often a parent. Police aren't surprised. They say they are seeing more and more parents willing to let teens drink at home, and parents will often supply the liquor. Parents say it's less risky than letting kids drink unsupervised.

Some people don't remember what they did when they were drunk, but often their friends do and may shun them for it.

make that person louder and less controlled. He or she may do loud or foolish things he or she would never do when sober.

That's what happened to Margaret. She got drunk at a party. She says the experience was so embarrassing, she won't be drinking again—at least not for a very long time.

"I sat in the lap of a guy I hardly knew," she says. "And then I felt really sick and threw up all over him. I didn't remember a whole lot about that night, but later when my friends told me what I'd done, I was like, 'I did what?' It's been a year, but I feel still feel embarrassed about it. And I can't look that boy in the eye when I see him in school."

But as painful as those experiences can be, there are other things that can happen when teens drink. And these things are far worse than embarrassing yourself in front of other people.

CHAPTER three

DRINKING CAN'T BE A MATTER OF LIFE AND DEATH, RIGHT?

Too much alcohol in your system definitely changes your behavior. It also affects your body and mind. These effects can lead you to perform risky, and even dangerous, behaviors.

The risk almost always centers upon your BAC, or blood-alcohol concentration. That's the number that indicates how much alcohol is in your bloodstream.

The higher the number, the more physical problems you exhibit. And the more likely you are to find yourself in a dangerous situation—even a life-threatening one. One of the most dangerous is driving drunk.

In the United States, it's a crime to drive with a BAC of 0.08 percent or higher. At that point, you are 25 percent more likely to have an accident than a sober driver.

Motor vehicle crashes are the number-one cause of death among youths ages 15 to 20.

But long before you get to that BAC level, the alcohol in your blood is having a huge effect on your body. At 0.02 percent, which is about one drink, your ability to concentrate is likely impaired. Driving requires you to concentrate on several things at the same time—to keep track of your speed, the side and rearview mirrors, your steering, and so on.

But if you are even slightly impaired at a 0.02 percent BAC, you may be so focused on checking your rearview mirror that you miss the fact that the stoplight up ahead has turned red. And your reaction to crossing over that center line may be slow and could endanger an oncoming car.

One man says that as a teenager, his drunkenness made him lose control of his motorcycle. He says that one of the worst decisions he's ever made was driving drunk. "I

19

Young drivers are less likely to use seat belts after they've been drinking, which leads to even more serious injuries and deaths.

was riding on my motorcycle and another car was coming toward me. I was feeling no pain, feeling so powerful and in control. As I came up on the car, it came into my lane slightly, and I overcorrected and went down. My foot was literally hanging by some cartilage. That foot still isn't right."

Binge Drinking

Another risky behavior is binge drinking. That's when you drink five or more drinks in a short period of time. Binge drinking is extremely dangerous, because your body cannot process the alcohol quickly enough. The alcohol enters the bloodstream and the brain. Drinking so much alcohol at one time interferes with the part of your brain that controls basic functions, including breathing and your gag reflex, which prevents you from choking.

This may cause you to pass out or lose consciousness. You may vomit while you're in this state and choke to death, because your gag reflex stops, too. Or you could simply stop breathing, which can happen when your BAC gets to 0.35 percent or above. When that happens, it's called alcohol poisoning.

"I woke up two hours later, not remembering anything about those two hours. I realized anything could have happened to me and I wouldn't have even known it."

One teen says a binge drinking incident made her stop drinking to excess. "I was at a party and just felt like getting really drunk. I got so drunk that I felt sick and wanted to be alone. I went outside, threw up, and laid down next to the house in the dark. I woke up two hours later, not remembering anything about those two hours. I realized anything could have happened to me and I wouldn't have even known it."

There are about 7 million teens who have engaged in binge drinking. In May 2008, a 16-year-old from Minnesota named Andrew Anderson was with two older brothers and a friend. He drank large amounts of vodka and passed out. Later he was found dead. His BAC was 0.353 percent. Ed Waltman,

Not Fun and Games

Drinking games have been linked to many episodes of underage binge drinking. The idea of a drinking game is always the same. The loser or losing team must drink entire glasses of beer or shots of liquor. The more you lose, the more drunk you become. The more drunk you become, the more likely you are to engage in risky behavior or to pass out.

Binge drinking can lead to a coma or even death. Nearly 19 percent of underage drinkers are binge drinkers.

superintendent of the community's schools, was frustrated and sad. "This [binge drinking] has been a huge concern for us," he said. "We have tried to do as much as we can ... but we need parents to talk to their children about not drinking."

Too Close to Dying

In Rohnert Park, California, a 15-year-old girl almost suffered the same fate. She was relaxing with friends in May 2008, and they all decided to drink vodka. After drinking about 13 shots, the girl wandered off to a park nearby. A while later, her friends found her passed out on a picnic table. When they couldn't wake her up, they called 911.

Dr. Barry Smith was the emergency room physician on duty that night at nearby Memorial Hospital. He was amazed that her BAC was a whopping 0.578. Usually a BAC that high is fatal, and he knew she was in trouble. "This little girl is the youngest [victim of alcohol poisoning] I had seen," he said.

The teen survived, but it was a very close call. Smith hopes that the girl's experience will be a warning to her friends and others that binge drinking can have serious consequences.

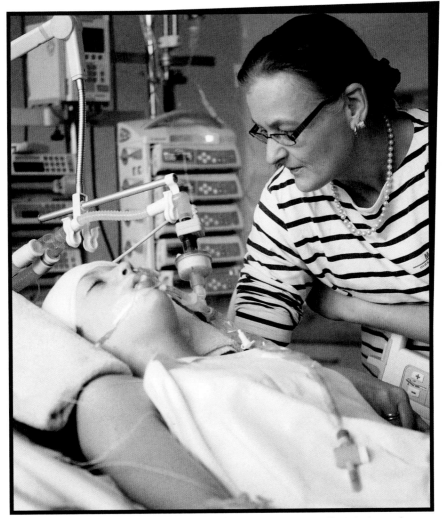

People who drink are four times more likely than nondrinkers to suffer injuries, such as falls. Binge drinkers are at even greater risk of hurting themselves.

"If they could see themselves having a tube being put down their throat, catheters [tubes inserted in your body to carry away urine] being put on, plugged into machines," he said, "if we could shock them, they might actually think, 'Boy, I really did almost die.'"

"We Thought We Were Bulletproof"

There are other dangers for underage drinkers, too. They are more inclined to engage in fights and risk pregnancy and sexually transmitted diseases (STDs) with unsafe sex. Their lack of judgment often results in risk-taking that they would rarely try sober.

One girl says that she often

The Danger Signs of Alcohol Poisoning

If someone you know has been drinking heavily and exhibits any of these signs, he or she may have alcohol poisoning:

- Mental confusion
- Vomiting
- Seizures
- Slow breathing (fewer than eight breaths per minute)
- Low body temperature
- Bluish or pale skin

If anyone exhibits any of these symptoms, call 911 or get him or her to an emergency room immediately.

More than half of 12th graders have admitted to being drunk at least once.

had sex when she drank. She says she didn't use good judgment, and she didn't think about birth control when she drank. She admits now that she often was so drunk that the next day she didn't remember having sex. She didn't even think about the danger of catching an STD. Months later, she had an outbreak of herpes. She doesn't know from whom she contracted the disease. What she does know is that drinking and lack of good judgment resulted in a problem that will last the rest of her life.

Suzanne says she and her friends also took risks when they binged. "We'd get wasted and go lie down on the railroad tracks outside of town," she remembers. "It was like a drinking game. We'd look to see if there was a light from an oncoming train, and if there was, we'd dare each other to lie down. It was like, how close can the train come before you get scared and roll off?"

She says she is ashamed of that part of her life. "It was so risky," she says. "And it was so stupid. What if we had gotten so drunk we passed out lying on the tracks? But we never thought about consequences. We thought we were bullet-proof, you know?"

The Sobering Facts

There are lots of myths out there about how to sober up fast when you've had too much to drink. Black coffee is one. Sleeping for a while is another. Taking a cold bath or shower is another. None of these methods work at all. "The only thing that reverses the effects of alcohol is time—something you may not have if you are suffering from alcohol poisoning," one expert says.

CHAPTER four

"IF I DON'T DRINK, I MIGHT AS WELL STAY HOME"

Knowing how dangerous drinking can be is one thing. But living in the real world is another. At parties especially, most teens feel pressure to fit in by drinking alcohol when others are doing so. Tessa says that as a teenager, she simply carried the same drink around at a party throughout the night.

"Friends at the party would ask if I wanted another drink, and I'd raise my glass and say, 'Got one, thanks.' No one really notices beyond that."

The Most Serious Pressure

Most underage drinkers say they started drinking because they felt pressured by friends. "It's huge. Peer pressure is one of the most common reasons why kids do anything," says Martha Nelson, who works with teen alcoholics and drug users. "When you're a teen, you're supposed to be pulling away from your parents—that's completely normal. The peer group often fills that role. But if the peer group is drinking, you'll drink."

John Gibbs, a substance abuse worker with at-risk teens, agrees but says that the pressure is not always obvious. "It's not a situation where kids come up and threaten other kids to drink. It's not 'You drink or else.' But if the goal for a kid is to be liked, to belong, he or she just observes what the peer group does. And then goes right along, doing the same."

Designated Driver

Andy has found a clever way to avoid the pressure to drink. "I'm not a drinker," he says. "But I like to go to parties. My parents trust me and told me that if I go, I could take the car and be the designated driver—the one whose job it is to drive all his drunk friends home afterward."

Andy says there have been good things about that role. One was that it made him feel good that his friends weren't driving. "They got home safe, and that was great," he says. "And the

"They got home safe, and that was great. And the other thing was, it gave me a good excuse not to drink."

other thing was, it gave me a good excuse not to drink."

He agrees that it's sometimes hard to refuse without sounding

Being a designated driver shows your parents you can be responsible.

27

like he disapproves of the ones who are drinking. "I'm not judging anybody," he says. "But you get a lot of weird looks, you know? People are like, 'What's wrong? Why don't you want a beer?' But now I can just say I'm the guy who's stuck driving everybody home, and that works." He admits that driving drinkers home has a bad side, too—having to clean up the backseat afterward. "Most of my friends don't get falling-down drunk," he says. "But a couple times, I've had someone who throws up in the back. The smell is terrible and hard to get out. That's the downside of being a designated driver."

The Costs Add Up!

There are many good reasons for a designated driver to be behind the wheel if you've been drinking. Not only is it safer, it makes the evening cheaper, too. According to Mothers Against Drunk Driving (MADD), the average cost for a first-offense drunken-driving case can be as much as $10,828:

- Minimum fine: $390
- Penalty assessment: $666
- State restitution fund: $100
- BAC testing fee: $37
- Jail and release fee: $10
- Required alcohol awareness school: $375
- License reissue fee: $100
- Attorney fees: $2,500
- Auto insurance increase: $3,600 to $6,600

Have a Good Reason Handy

There are lots of ways to say no to a drink. You don't have to sound like you are rejecting your friends. "Since high school, I've usually had a couple of good ones handy," says Nora. "Like, 'Oh, thanks, but my soccer coach would bench me,' or 'Can't. I've got a game, and we've got team rules.' Something like that."

How to Say No to Alcohol (and Not Feel Like an Outsider):

1. Say you haven't eaten, and you don't want to get drunk.
2. Tell them alcoholism runs in your family, and you'd rather not risk it.
3. If you're not feeling brave about saying no, just blame your parents or coach. Say they'll ground you, get mad, or kick you off the team if you drink.
4. Say the party is so much fun, you don't need to drink.
5. Tell them you've had a bad experience drinking in the past, and you'd rather not repeat it.

The average age that American teens begin drinking regularly is 15.9 years, but drinking as a teen is risky. Not only is it illegal, it also puts the person at greater risk of becoming an alcoholic and developing other serious health issues.

She has to be a bit more creative now that she's in college. "I say that I'm tired, and a drink would put me right to sleep," she says. "I tell them I just want to enjoy the party. Or I just say I'm not ready yet, but maybe later. Whatever works—and the thing is, if I feel too pressured, I just leave that party."

The Quiet Brain

As recently as 2007, studies are producing some scary information about the dangers of early drinking. Teens who drink are more at risk for brain damage than adults who drink. That's because the teen brain is still growing and forming. Alcohol can interfere with the brain's growth and how well it functions. One interesting visual is the scan of two brains—one of a 15-year-old drinker and the other of a 15-year-old non-drinker. Activity in the brain shows up as bright red blotches. There are plenty in the nondrinker's scan. But the drinker's brain shows almost no red at all—it seems perfectly quiet.

Beyond Excuses

That brings up another option. If you get tired of making excuses not to drink, you may have to change who you hang out with. If you find yourself slipping into the same old pattern of drinking and partying when you don't want to, are your friends that good for you?

Suzanne says she has learned that because drinking was one of her friends' favorite activities, she often ended up drinking when she hung out with them. She would start out the evening promising that she wouldn't drink. But her friends wouldn't let her get away with not joining in. "They would be like, 'Come on, Suz, just one,' or something like that. I'm not saying it was their fault. It wasn't. It was my fault. But I wasn't strong enough to say no to them. My life would have gotten better a whole lot faster if I had."

> "It was my fault. But I wasn't strong enough to say no to them. My life would have gotten better a whole lot faster if I had."

Patty Griffith, a psychologist who works with chemically dependent teens, knows how important friends are. "I would urge someone who doesn't really want to drink to change his or her peer group," she says. "Don't hand over the decisions about parties and activities like that to people who don't share your interests. Be a planner yourself; make your own decisions about what you like to do."

Griffith says that many teens feel the same way. "Look around," she says. "There are probably lots of other kids who aren't [alcohol] users, kids who are into a healthier lifestyle. And if you don't think you could be a leader, be a follower—find a group that isn't drinking, and start hanging out with them."

Three More Reasons Not to Drink as a Teen

1. The rate of fatal car crashes among underage drinkers is twice that of drinkers 21 and over.
2. Thirty-seven percent of eighth-grade girls who drink heavily admitted to having attempted suicide.
3. Teens who drink are far more likely to engage in high-risk sex, especially multiple partners or unprotected sex.

Though it may seem as if everyone drinks, that isn't true. Look closer, and you'll find others who share your values and want to stay away from alcohol.

CHAPTER five

I THINK I HAVE A PROBLEM

One of the most troubling effects of underage drinking is that it can turn into alcoholism. Studies show that the earlier people begin to drink the more likely they are to become alcoholics.

Do you have a drinking problem? Experts say there are several warning signs that someone has a drinking problem and may be in danger of becoming addicted to alcohol:

- You feel like you need a drink when you are upset.
- You prefer to drink when you're by yourself.
- You hide how much you're drinking from your friends and family.
- You often feel as if you need a drink at school or at work.
- You keep a bottle hidden somewhere, just in case you need it.
- You find it impossible to stop drinking, or even to cut back on your drinking.

If you are drinking at school or hiding your drinking, you need to seek help right away.

I Wish I'd Listened to Myself

Suzanne says that by the time she was 14, those warning signs all sounded familiar. "I read an article in a magazine about teenage drinkers, and I knew right away they could have been using my name," she says. "And really, I could have written a few more warning signs."

Jerry also says he knew he was an alcoholic at an early age, and he was always drunk or high. He says that the first time he went to Alcoholics Anonymous (A.A.) was when he was 16, after a drunken fall out of a tree perforated his kidney.

"I knew I had almost died. I fell 25 feet. I went to an

Breath Testing in Schools

Some schools test students with a breathalyzer to cut back on underage drinking at school or school events. When a person blows into the device, it can measure his or her BAC. By 2007, the sale of breathalyzers to U.S. high schools had risen 120 percent.

A.A. meeting. But when I sat there, it just sounded like something I couldn't do. They were offering God as a solution, but I knew that I wanted to keep drinking. I couldn't relate. I tried going again when I was 18 and thought the same thing. Finally, when I was 21, A.A. started making sense. By then, I hadn't had a sober day in years."

Jerry had friends who knew he had a problem, but he couldn't find a way to change. "Alcohol helped me cope. I couldn't figure out what I would do without it."

"Finally, when I was 21, A.A. started making sense. By then, I hadn't had a sober day in years."

Getting Help

Jerry's story is very common. Often it's only after a teen gets in trouble with the law that he or she gets professional help to

Alcohol-treatment programs often include group therapy, when teens can talk about their problems with other teens.

*If someone you love is an alcoholic, you may need counseling yourself.
Don't be afraid to ask for help if you need it.*

stop drinking. Corey was arrested for drunk driving and had to pay a heavy fine. In addition, he was ordered into treatment by the court.

Corey started his treatment at an inpatient clinic with other teens who had drinking problems.

Places like this have counselors and health workers who can closely monitor the residents. It's important that each teen gets sober, to clean out all of the toxins in the body. So it's really important that nobody sneaks drugs or alcohol into the clinic.

Dirty UA?

One tool health professionals use to monitor a teen is urine analysis, or UA. By examining the urine sample, the lab can tell whether the teen has had any alcohol within the past few days. If a teen's UA is "dirty"—meaning it shows alcohol use—he or she is often sent back to inpatient care for more intense treatment.

Survival Skills

If you're a teen in alcohol treatment, learning not to drink is the least of your problems. Your whole way of looking at yourself and your life needs to change. That's where counselors and therapists come in. They can help you figure out ways to live without drinking. They can help you learn to control the urge to use alcohol when you're upset or stressed.

Social worker Jane Schwark works with teens in a juvenile detention facility. She says that teaching kids to live without alcohol is one of the most important aspects of her job. "We often role play—teaming up two kids, sitting back to back," she says. "One tries to get the other to start using [alcohol], and the other practices ways to refuse. It's a good exercise, because these kids are going to be living that

A trusted adult can help you find the resources you need if you or a loved one is battling alcoholism.

dilemma when they get back to their normal lives."

When counselors feel that the teens can function with less daily intervention, they can move to outpatient care. They can begin living at home while continuing their therapy and counseling sessions. Many attend meetings of a group such as A.A., which can help them talk about the difficulty of staying sober.

"Treatment and A.A. basically changed my life," Corey says. "When I first got out of residential care, I went to 60 meetings [of A.A.] in 60 days. I thought at first I'd hate it, but it was great. I've got an A.A. sponsor, a guy I can call 24/7, whenever I feel like I'm going to drink. He's been a lifesaver for me."

Life Is Good

Of course, if you have a drinking problem, staying sober is going to be tough. There will be all kinds of pressures you'll feel that will make you want to go back to using alcohol. Psychologists call these triggers—situations that can make you feel that you

Dealing With Triggers

Teens need to have tools ready to fight the stresses that trigger their drinking. "It could be stress at school, or parents fighting, or feeling pressure from friends," says Jane Schwark, a juvenile detention treatment worker. "And those triggers are not going anywhere. So kids have to learn survival skills to combat those triggers. For example, when they feel that stress, they could grab a basketball and go to the park to shoot hoops for awhile. Or maybe there's a neighbor who's nice, and the teenager could go over there and hang out. Whatever works."

need to drink. It's very common for teens to relapse, or slide back into drinking.

But with time and determination, many alcoholics have learned to deal with those triggers. They find they can manage the stress in their lives without drinking. Corey says it's been a tough battle for him, but he's proud of what he's accomplished. "Life is good," he says. "I don't ever think I've felt that way in a long time. But things are so much better sober."

Good friends can be your greatest allies. Friends who make good choices can help you make good choices, too.

QUIZ

The following true or false questions can help you discover
how savvy you are about alcohol use.

1. Drinking with friends is not a problem, since we can
take care of one another.

2. The more you weigh, the more you can drink without
getting drunk.

3. Drinking is one of those things every teenager does,
like a rite of passage.

4. If your date offers you a beer, it's OK to say no.

5. If you must drive after drinking, go very slow, so you
don't hurt anyone.

Answers:

1. False. You may think that's a good plan, but as you drink
   more and more, you are less able to make judgments about
   how to help yourself, let alone be a help to your friends.

2. True and False. It's true that people who weigh more can usually
   drink more without feeling the effects of alcohol. But other
   factors, like not having eaten recently, may make a bigger person
   just as susceptible to getting drunk as a smaller person would be.

3. False. It's true that many teens try it, but many teens believe
   it makes sense to wait until they are 21.

4. True: Many teens say that it can actually make them more relaxed
   if their date isn't interested in drinking.

5. False, False, False! It's never OK to drive when you've been
   drinking. You can get into as much trouble going slowly as you
   can when you're speeding. Your judgment and reactions are
   impaired, and you will be a danger to yourself and others.

GLOSSARY

alcoholic | someone who is addicted to drinking alcohol

alcohol poisoning | possibly fatal condition when a dangerous amount of alcohol is consumed

binge drinking | when a person drinks five or more alcoholic beverages in one sitting

blackout | state caused by drinking in which a person may still function but can't remember anything

blood-alcohol concentration | level of alcohol in one's bloodstream

central nervous system | brain and spinal cord

gag reflex | automatic reaction that forces you to cough and prevents you from choking to death

relapse | slide back into unwanted behavior

sober | unimpaired by alcohol or drugs

toxin | poison

trigger | something or someone that sets off a process; in the case of drinking, a trigger is something that makes you want to drink

WHERE TO GET HELP

Al-Anon/Alateen
Al-Anon Family Groups Headquarters
Virginia Beach, VA 23454-5617
757/536-1600
Al-Anon is made up of people whose lives have been affected by a family member who is an alcohol abuser. Alateen is made up primarily of teenagers who are affected. These groups hold meetings to share experiences and offer support to one another. Use the Web site, www.al-anon.alateen.org, to find upcoming meetings in your area.

Alcoholics Anonymous
A.A. World Services, Inc.
P.O. Box 459
New York, NY 10163
212/870-3400
This worldwide organization is for recovering alcoholics. They work to remain sober, using a 12-step program that stresses responsibility and the need for reconciling with those they have hurt along the way. You can go to A.A.'s Web site, www.aa.org, to find meetings near you, as well as get information that can help you decide whether A.A. is likely to work for you.

Choose Responsibility
P.O. Box 507
Middlebury, VT 05753
802/398-2024
Choose Responsibility is a nonprofit organization founded in 2007 to raise awareness of reckless drinking by young people. You can learn more about binge drinking, drinking and driving, and other safety issues by going to its Web site, www.chooseresponsibility.org.

Mothers Against Drunk Driving
MADD National Office
Irving, TX 75062
800/438-6233
MADD seeks to be the voice of victims of drunk-driving accidents. The organization arranges speaking engagements to businesses, schools, and other community groups. It also provides educational materials for drivers' education programs.

National Center on Addiction and Substance Abuse
633 Third Ave.
New York, NY 10017-6706
212/841-5200
CASA works to organize professionals in many disciplines—law enforcement, psychology, and biomedical research—to get to the root of combating alcohol abuse. Its Web site, www.casacolumbia.org, has links to current articles and information that can help if you're doing research for a school report.

National Clearinghouse for Alcohol & Drug Information
P.O. Box 2345
Rockville, MD 20847-2345
800/729-6686
NCADI is the world's largest resource for information on alcohol and other drugs. The organization distributes brochures, pamphlets, and videotapes to families, schools, and professionals to educate them on the need for better control of abused substances. Call or write to them, and they can give you information on drinking and its effects.

SOURCE NOTES

Chapter 1
Page 5, column 1, line 1: Nora. South Bend, Ind. Telephone interview. 24 June 2008.
Page 5, column 2, line 5: Ibid.
Page 8, column 2, line 5: Jerry. Atlanta, Ga. Telephone interview. 2 Sept. 2008.
Page 10, column 2, line 1: Corey. Richfield, Minn. Personal interview. 10 June 2008.
Page 11, column 2, line 2: Martha Nelson. St. Paul, Minn. Telephone interview. 16 July 2008.

Chapter 2
Page 12, line 9: Theo. Minneapolis, Minn. Personal interview. 14 May 2008.
Page 13, column 1, line 1: Corey.
Page 17, column 1, line 11: Nelson.

Chapter 3
Page 19, column 2, line 14: Jerry.
Page 21, column 2, line 3: Tessa. San Francisco, Calif. Personal interview. 2 Sept. 2008.
Page 22, column 1, line 3: Heron Marquez Estrada. "Mankato Again Loses a Young Life to Alcohol." *StarTribune*, Minneapolis. 1 June 2008, p. A1.
Page 22, column 2, line 10: Laura Norton. "Perils of Teen Drinking." *The Press Democrat*, Santa Rosa, Calif. 10 May 2008, p. A1.
Page 23, column 1, line 1: Ibid.
Page 25, sidebar: "Facts About Alcohol Poisoning." College Drinking Prevention. http://www.collegedrinkingprevention.gov/OtherAlcoholInformation/factsAboutAlcoholPoisoning.aspx
Page 25, column 2, line 6: Suzanne. Minneapolis. Personal interview. 14 June 2008.
Page 25, column 2, line 19: Ibid.

Chapter 4
Page 26, line 12: Tessa.
Page 26, line 22: Nelson.
Page 27, column 1, line 5: John Gibbs. Minneapolis. Personal interview. 14 Sept. 2008.
Page 27, column 1, line 17: Andy. Hinsdale, Ill. Telephone interview. 6 July 2008.
Page 27, column 2, line 2: Ibid.
Page 28, column 1, line 2: Ibid.
Page 28, column 2, line 8: Ibid.
Page 28, column 2, line 21: Nora.
Page 31, column 1, line 3: Ibid.
Page 31, column 2, line 25: Suzanne.
Page 32, column 1, line 11: Dr. Patty Griffith. Minneapolis. Telephone interview. 9 July 2008.
Page 32, column 1, line 22: Ibid.

Chapter 5
Page 35, column 2, line 1: Suzanne.
Page 36, column 2, line 6: Jerry.
Page 37, column 2, line 3: Ibid.
Page 40, column 1, line 25: Jane Schwark. Hastings, Minn. Telephone interview. 10 July 2008.
Page 41, column 1, line 13: Corey.
Page 41, sidebar: Schwark.
Page 42, column 2, line 4: Corey.

Fiction

Day, Karen. *Tall Tales*. New York: Wendy Lamb Books, 2007.

Fogelin, Adrian. *The Sorta Sisters*. Atlanta: Peachtree, 2007.

Luddy, Karon. *Spelldown*. New York: Simon & Schuster Books for Young Readers, 2007.

Nonfiction

Connolly, Sean. *Alcohol*. North Mankato, Minn.: Smart Apple Media, 2007.

Kittleson, Mark, ed. *The Truth About Alcohol*. New York: Facts on File, 2005.

Lynette, Rachel. *Alcohol*. Chicago: Heinemann Library, 2008.

R., John (anonymous). *Big Book Unplugged: A Young Person's Guide to Alcoholics Anonymous*. Center City, Minn.: Hazelden, 2003.

Walker, Ida. *Alcohol Addiction: Not Worth the Buzz*. Philadelphia: Mason Crest Publishers, 2008.

Wyborny, Sheila. *Alcoholism*. Detroit: Lucent Books, 2008.

For more information on this topic, use FactHound.

1. Go to *www.facthound.com*

2. Choose your grade level.

3. Begin your search.

This book's ID number is 9780756541514

FactHound will find the best sites for you.

INDEX

ABOUT THE AUTHOR

Gail Stewart has written more than 240 books for children and teens. She has written extensively on drug and alcohol abuse among young people. She received her undergraduate degree from Gustavus Adolphus College in St. Peter, Minnesota. After teaching junior high English and reading for 10 years, she did graduate work at the University of Minnesota and the University of St. Thomas. She lives in Minneapolis, Minnesota.

ABOUT THE CONTENT ADVISER

Billy AraJeJe Woods has a doctorate in psychology, a master's in education, and a bachelor's in psychology. He has been counseling individuals and families for more than 25 years. He is a certified transactional analysis counselor and a drug and alcohol abuse counselor. A professor of psychology at Saddleback College, Mission Viejo, California, Woods teaches potential counselors to work with dysfunctional families and special populations. He began his counseling career in the military where he worked with men and women suffering from post-traumatic stress disorder. In his practice, Woods has worked with many young adults on issues related to drug and alcohol abuse and body image.